Level 3 Diploma Health and Social Care– An easy to read guide

By Kelsey Allsopp

CONTENTS

Author-Kelsey Allsopp

Copyright 2012 by Kelsey Allsopp

SECTION 1

WHY THE DIPLOMA?

WHAT IS THE L3 DIPLOMA AND WHY DO I HAVE TO DO IT?

This is one of the first questions that carers normally ask when notified that they have to start the Diploma. Many people, particularly those with degrees or professional qualifications, feel that it is not relevant to them and that they are overqualified or already show adequate evidence of their standards of work. There are many different reasons why it is vital to complete a Diploma: -

1. At present there is a Legislative requirement that 50% of Care staff on each working shift hold or are working towards a Level 2 qualification or above. New employees are expected to complete a work induction within 12 weeks of employment and to have started the qualification within 6 months.

2. By 2007, 80% of staff in each care home must hold or be working towards level 2 or above. Registered managers must hold a Health and Social Care level 5 qualification which will replace the old registered managers award.

3. By undertaking a qualification that is directly related to the place of work and where evidence is gathered through real work activities, it is felt that the result will be to produce staff who feel more confident in their work, provide a higher standard of care and have good knowledge and understanding of important legislation and organisational policies that inform practice. Candidates can also present this evidence to other employers to show they can carry out certain activities, and have significant knowledge about the legal requirements that inform the work they undertake.

4. The process can also help identify any weak area's that a candidate needs training in i.e. health and safety, child protection and also any basic skills that the candidate needs extra support with. Many Assessors are now being trained to tutor candidates in basic skills for English and Math's if needed, as part of the package. This can be of particular use to those whose first language is not English.

Therefore, if candidates apply themselves to their work and are committed to the process there is a wide range of learning opportunities. I have never personally assessed a candidate who felt they had learnt nothing from completing their qualification. Many candidates say that they never realised how much they knew until they were required to show evidence of it, and also express concern about how little knowledge they had of legal and organisational requirements that should be informing the way they work. This demonstrates that although the qualification can be time consuming, it has valid relevance to the care duties and practice we undertake in the here and now.

HOW LONG WILL THE DIPLOMA TAKE, AND WHAT'S IN IT FOR ME

A Diploma generally takes between 9 – 12 months to complete if the candidate is committed to the process and makes good use of their Assessor time. Most Diploma providers, however, usually allow up to 18 months for completion. If for some reason i.e. long-term sickness, the candidate cannot feasibly complete within the time limit then the Diploma provider can authorise an extension. Bear in mind though that there must be very good reasons for an extension, and the Diploma provider may charge extra for this.

Some of the positive reasoning for completing a Diploma was presented earlier. You will develop a clearer knowledge of what you know, and learn about important legislation and organisational policies that will inform the way you practice. You will also build up a portfolio that shows evidence of how you apply what you know to the way you practice. This can be very useful not just for now but to show future employers.

You will also be obtaining a recognised qualification in your field of work and some companies, although not all, show recognition of this through related pay awards and bonus schemes.

The Diploma is a work-related and competence based qualification and is based on national occupational standards. The standards set describe what competent people in their area of work should be able to do. It demonstrates the skills and knowledge that are required to ensure best practice, and that you (the candidate) are competent in the area of work that your Diploma covers.

SECTION 2

STARTING YOUR PORTFOLIO

INITIAL PAPERWORK

This is a list of all the initial paperwork your portfolio should have and what each is used for. The pages are listed in order (so the 1st listed page should be at the front of your file and so on) and after the list are copies of some the pages so you know roughly what they all look like.

1. Summary of achievement. This form is where your Assessor lists all the units you are completing to make up your award. Every time you send a unit in to be internally verified both you and your assessor will sign next to the appropriate unit to say it is complete and to state which types of evidence you used the most to complete it. There is a space for the Internal verifier (IV) to sign. The IV will only sign if they agree, after going through it, that the unit is completed satisfactorily. Occasionally a visiting External verifier, whose job it is to ensure that Assessors and Internal verifiers are doing their part correctly, will also sign on this line to show that they agree with the assessment decision. Your Diploma provider will tell you their centre number and your enrolment number so you can fill these parts in.

2. Induction checklist. Your Diploma provider will have a duty to make you aware of certain policies and procedures before you start i.e. complaints procedure. These are all written on an induction checklist and your Assessor will tick each one as they have explained it to you and given you any relevant paperwork.

3. Health and social care Diploma Internal Verification checklist. This document is for your information. It shows a general checklist of what the Internal Verifier is looking for when they go through your completed work.

4. Confidentiality policy. This will detail your providers' policies on the information they hold about you and how they are allowed or not allowed to use it.

5. Plagiarism statement. This explains what plagiarism is, how to avoid it and your providers policy on dealing with it.

6. Policy and Procedures. Your provider should give you a document that details how the provider will monitor the candidate's progress, meetings with Assessors and also the appeals procedure and the role of the Assessor.

7. Appeals Procedure. This document explains the appeals procedure in full.

8. Data protection Policy. This covers legislation that dictates how your information can be used or not used.

9. Learner feedback on assessor performance. This is normally to be filled in by yourself half way through your award to give constructive feedback on your Assessors work with you.

10. Candidate and Centre Details. This form holds information about the award you are doing, your contact details and your providers' details.

11. Contact details and signatures. This form has details of how your Assessor can be contacted and also your contact details and your line Managers.

12. Candidate Resume. This is basically for you to record your qualifications and experience to date. Some are fairly basic. Others require a full CV. If you already have a full CV you can include this instead.

13. Assessment process for Diploma's in Health and Social Care. This form explains all the types of evidence used and other paperwork relevant to the unit.

14. Skill Scan. Some providers and organisations require that candidate's carry out skills scan so they can ascertain which Diploma they are best suited to. They usually involve writing a short assignment relevant to a part of the Diploma.

SECTION 3

DIPLOMA EVIDENCE

WHAT DO I NEED IT FOR?

PERFORMANCE CRITERIA/LEARNING OUTCOMES. WHAT IS IT? HOW DO I COVER IT?

Performance Criteria or Learning Outcomes (known as PC'S) are a list of practices that you must show that you:

a) Complete or have completed within your work.

OR

b) That you demonstrate sufficient knowledge to the Assessor to prove you understand what the task would entail and would be able to carry it out.

Performance Criteria/Learning outcomes range from demonstrating that you are mindful of infection control when you administer medication to being able to respond to a client's disclosure of abuse. You can use a variety of evidence to prove your competence in each Pc (the types of evidence will be explained fully later) and often one piece of evidence can cover a number of Pc's within one unit

Example of how to cover a Pc:

Pc 1- you monitor working area's to ensure they are safe and free from hazards.

Covering this Pc could be as simple as asking a colleague to watch you at work while you are carrying out health and safety checks around your workplace and then writing a short statement to say that they have seen you doing this. This evidence would be called a witness statement.

The Performance criteria or Learning outcome for a unit will also require you demonstrate knowledge of the systems that inform your practice.
Through knowledge you should be able to identify the important pieces of legislation and organisational policy that inform all your practice. A lot of the information you need for the legislation knowledge requirements can be found in the Care Standards Act 2000, which there should be a copy of in your workplace. Similarly to find knowledge regarding your organisations practices you should have in your workplace a policies and procedures file giving you most of the information you need.
As a guideline, if the Learning outcome asks you to demonstrate, this will be covered by witness statements and/or direct observation. If it asks you to identify

or explain then this will require you to write a piece yourself and this is where your knowledge of policies, procedure and legislation is likely to be required.

SECTION 4

DIFFERENT TYPES OF EVIDENCE

EVIDENCE

Direct Observations- These are written by your assessor. They will make arrangements with you to come and observe you in your workplace. They may do a holistic observation where you are observed for a few hrs or more in your normal work, or they may come especially to observe something specific i.e. you administrating medication. In either case your assessor will go away and write up their observation and work out what performance criteria or knowledge they have observed you carry out. A holistic observation generally covers more learning outcomes and knowledge because you may carry out several different activities relating to the unit you are working on. An observation of a specific task may cover half or more of 1 unit.

Witness statements/Testimony- Witness statements are gathered by you. They are written by colleagues or other people you meet in your work. When you are witnessed by someone carrying out specific work activities (your assessor will identify some of these activities with you) that person can write a short witness statement to say what work they saw you undertake. This can then be used as evidence to cover Learning outcomes and knowledge requirements.

Work products- These are written by you. Some assessors call them **Reflective accounts**. They are both the same thing so don't get confused. They are pieces of work written by you demonstrating that you know what to do in certain situations. For example, you may write a work product explaining the procedures you would follow in the event that someone told you they had been abused (disclosure). The length of Work products will depend on your own style of writing and the amount of learning outcomes and knowledge you are covering within the piece.

Professional Discussion- These take place with your assessor. If, for example you have not had the opportunity in your work to carry out a specific activity or it is not something that could be easily witnessed by someone, i.e. that you build up good therapeutic relationships with those you care for, then you may have a professional discussion with your assessor to explain how you do these things.

Question and answers/questioning – These also take place with your assessor. They will ask you specific questions about your work practice and record your answers.

Certificates-Any certificates you have of related training should be photocopied and the copy kept in your Diploma portfolio/folder. These are especially useful if you can include with them the different area's the course/qualification covered. Your Assessor will identify with you the specific relevance of each course to your Diploma.

All the evidence above is stored in separate sections in your Diploma file. After the initial paperwork at the beginning of your file, you will need to create 8 sections for the following evidence. It is best to use dividers to do this. The sections are: -

1. Observations
2. Witness statements
3. Work products/Reflective Accounts
4. Professional Discussion
5. Question and Answers
6. Certificates
7. Review and Action Plans
8. Unit Feedback Sheet

Sections 1 – 6 are for your evidence, which have been explained above. Section 7 is for your Review and Action Plans. Every time your assessor meets with you they will write on a review and action plan, a brief account of what you have planned or covered during your meeting and what will be happening next. Section 8 is for unit feedback sheets. When you have completed a unit your assessor fills in a unit feedback sheet to give feedback and advice to you about your Diploma work. You will then be asked to comment on what they have written and to sign it. The whole unit is then submitted for Internal Verification. Some Diploma providers will use their own computer system for monitoring and storing your work. Don't be fazed by this. The systems are easy to use even if you have no prior IT experience, and you will learn new IT skills on the way.

Example of a Direct Observation * = A NAME

I observed * today at * House which is her place of work. Before administering medication * went into the clinic and checked that there was plenty of water, medication pots and that the surfaces and equipment were clean. * also washed her hands as part of Infection control. When the client came to have her medication * checked that she knew who the client was. * then got the client's medication from a locked safe. * checked the medication label against the medication administration record ………… and so on.

The observation will be written on specific paperwork, which your assessor has, and the Learning outcomes and knowledge the observation covers will be listed down the right hand side. The above observation would most likely be used for unit 116 Support use of Medication in Social care settings. This is only a small example but it already demonstrates that the candidate is aware of infection control (they washed their hands and checked surfaces were clean) and that they check the identity of the individual (to avoid hazards).
I have not shown an example of a Witness Testimony, as these are very similar to the observation. The only differences are that they are written and signed by someone other than your assessor, and they are written on different paper work that your assessor will give you. Your assessor will initially identify with you the area's that need covering by witness statements but as you progress through the Diploma you should be able to do this for yourself.

Example of a work product

In my workplace there are 8 clients who I care for. As my organisation uses an individualistic approach this requires me to work in a way that acknowledges and respects the differences and diversity between people. I practice this by making sure I am aware of differences in Care plans, by being non-judgemental towards people with different religious or cultural beliefs…….. and so on.

The work product will be written by you and there is no specific paperwork. Normal A4 paper will do. The above work product would be used specifically to a unit requiring information about the theories behind your work practice or about how you work within the guidelines of The Equal Opportunities or Anti-

Discrimination acts. Your assessor will give you an idea of the information to be included within your work products and will always check any evidence that you or someone else writes to check where it fits within your Diploma requirements.

Example of a Professional Discussion

* = NAME

* and I had a professional discussion about Child Protection procedures that are applicable to her working practice. We discussed the symptoms and signs of abuse and how * would respond to these. * said that through her yearly mandatory Child Protection Training she has learnt to look for the following signs of emotional, physical and sexual abuse ……… and so on.
This Professional Discussion would be relevant to the unit 25 Understand how to safeguard the wellbeing of Children and young people. For those studying Health and Social care Adults the discussion would be around S.O.V.A (safeguarding of vulnerable adults) training and procedures, which are very similar. Your assessor will write up Professional Discussions on specific paperwork and discuss with you what evidence you have covered.

Example of question and answers

Q. What are the arrangements for storage of different types of Medication in your workplace?

A. All medication is kept in a locked clinic. The keys to this clinic are kept in a locked office that only staff have access to. Medication is stored in the following ways in the clinic: -

Controlled drugs i.e. tamazepan is kept in a separate locked safe. 2 people, when dispensing must complete the doses and signatures for this medication. Temperature controlled medication is kept in 2 locked fridges and the temperatures are checked and recorded at each administration time to check they are within the limits.
…….. and so on.

This evidence clearly links to the knowledge specification for unit 116 where the Diploma candidate is asked to demonstrate that they know certain information about the storage of medication. Your assessor will ask the question and write it, and your answer on specific paper work for Question and Answer evidence, and then discuss with you what evidence requirements you have covered within it.

The bulk of your evidence will come from Direct Observations and Witness Statements. Direct Observations are obviously a strong type of evidence and most units require a certain amount of your evidence to be covered using them. The thought of putting together enough evidence to complete just one unit may appear daunting, but it is not as hard as it may first appear. A Direct Observation and a Witness Testimony may typically cover a third to half of 1 unit. It is not until your assessor explains what they are looking for you to evidence, that you will begin to realise exactly how much you have already done, know and can demonstrate.

SECTION 5

YOUR ASSESSOR AND INTERNAL VERIFIER

YOUR DIPLOMA ASSESSOR

Your Diploma Assessor is your first call for support. Their role is to help you put together work-based evidence that will demonstrate practice and knowledge in your field of work, and that reach the national occupational standards of competency.

Your Assessor will meet with you a minimum of once a month. They will probably set you work to do between meetings and will keep a record of progress made and of what you cover in your meetings (see Action and Review Plans). Your Assessor will also be available for telephone contact between meetings if you need help and support.

Your Assessor will come out to your workplace at times arranged between you, to observe your work practice. They can then say in their written observations, that what they have observed reaches the national occupational standards. They will also check any evidence you provide, i.e. work products and witness statements, to make sure it completely fits/covers the related learning outcomes. The Assessor will write up any Direct Observations that take place as well as the Professional Discussions and records of Questioning. They will then record on these pieces of evidence, which Performance Criteria and Knowledge Specification they cover.

When you begin your Diploma your Assessor will give you your first unit. You need to create a separate section for each unit in your folder after the evidence sections. Again, dividers are handy. The first few pages of the unit detail the title and number of the unit with the elements of competence. These pages give you information about what they are looking for you to show evidence of and what certain terms within the unit mean. Read these carefully to avoid confusion.

The learning outcomes are then split up into assessment criteria i.e. for unit 051: -

The unit is called Promote communication in Health, Social Care or Children and young people's settings.

The aims of the unit are explained and the learning outcomes listed. The following pages of the unit list the assessment criteria for each outcome. In unit 051 there are 4 learning outcomes. There are then 2 assessment criteria in order to cover Outcome 1, 4 assessment criteria for outcome 2 and so on.

Next there is a list of evidence requirements. These outline the types of evidence that will be most appropriate to this unit, and any difficulties they predict you will come across.

Lastly there are, what we call, Ticky Boxes. These are sheets, one per **outcome** i.e. one for 051 Outcome i, one for 051 Outcome 2 and so on. Every time a piece of evidence is complete the Assessor will give it a page number i.e. Witness Testimony page 2, and write it on the Ticky box sheet. Then she will tick the boxes next to it to say which assessment criteria the evidence covers. This is so the IV can look at the Ticky box sheet and see, for example, that witness testimony page 2 covers Assessment criteria 2,3 and 4 and then find the witness testimony page 2 and check that it does in fact cover these criteria.

Your Assessors role is to go through the unit with you initially, explaining what evidence you will need to use and what evidence they will directly observe themselves. Their job is to make sure that every Learning outcome is covered before they hand the file in for IV. If parts have been missed the IV will hand the file back to the Assessor as not passed, and you will have to gather further evidence before sending it back for IV again. Depending on how often the IV days are held, this can be time consuming so it is best that you check and double check work yourself before handing it to the Assessor. The Assessor will be there throughout the whole of your Diploma to guide and advise you. They will give specific feedback on each unit, and make you aware of any extra training you might need to do.

YOUR INTERNAL VERIFIER

You will probably not have cause to meet the Internal Verifier (IV) unless problems arise with your work or your Assessor. They are there to monitor the Assessment procedures in relation to the National occupational Standards. The IV monitors the work that the Assessor carries out with you to ensure that your work is meeting the standards required. On IV days the IV will go through the units(s) handed in to check that the Assessment process has been completed fully and your unit does indeed meet the required standards by covering all the Outcomes and Knowledge requirements completely. They will also be looking at the Review and Action plans to ensure the Assessor has shown adequate planning for the units and at the unit feedback sheet to see that they have given full and applicable feedback. The IV then writes a short report for you and the Assessor. If they feel the unit is incomplete then they will give details of what has not been covered, how it should be covered and any problems with the Assessors planning and feedback. The amendments will then need to be made so the unit can be IV'D again. If they consider the unit to be complete they will say so in their report and sign the summary of achievement form therefore passing the unit.

COMMON MISTAKES AND HOW TO AVOID THEM

1. Knowledge – This is where the most mistakes and omissions occur. If you have a knowledge pack for a unit it will have a series of questions to answer. After each question it will say what knowledge the question covers. Check the question against the Diploma knowledge requirements to check that a. it makes sense and b. as guidance on what information it is vital to get into your answer. This sounds daft but sometimes mistakes are made by those creating the knowledge packs. When checking through your completed unit check the Knowledge requirements v carefully. This is really tedious and time consuming but will ensure you have not missed anything. Most of the time files are sent back because of missing Knowledge requirements as opposed to learning outcomes because the evidence for the outcomes is bigger and clearly structured.

2. When writing evidence yourself explain what it is you have done as though you are writing it for someone who has no care experience. Make sure that any 'care language' you use is fully explained. For example the word 'POST' won't mean anything to anyone without eating disorder experience. I would need to explain that post is a set period of time directly after a client has eaten where they must remain sitting, under staff observation so that they do not have opportunity to vomit or exercise. Be very specific in what you are trying to convey within the evidence.

3. Let your Assessor fill in the Ticky Box sheet. If you do it yourself and make a mistake then the sheets can end up looking messy and confuse the IV. The same goes for evidence. Let the Assessor write on, which learning outcomes and knowledge the evidence covers so to avoid confusion and messy work.

4. If possible type your work products and save them on to disc. This makes it easy to add to them or alter, if necessary.

SECTION 6

THE MANDATORY UNITS

HSC 051: – PROMOTE COMMUNICATION IN HEALTH, SOCIAL CARE OR CHILDREN'S AND YOUNG PEOPLE'S SETTINGS

Unit 051- PROMOTE EFFECTIVE COMMUNICATION IN HEALTH, SOCIAL CARE OR CHILDREN AND YOUNG PEOPLE'S SETTINGS

About the unit – This unit has 4 Learning outcomes, all requiring evidence of your knowledge and ability to communicate and receive communications. Some of the issues to be communicated may be sensitive, and others quite simple or typical. You will also be required to demonstrate that you know how to read, access and update records/reports, following the correct procedures particularly around confidentiality. Communication means a variety of different things in this unit. It can include verbal and non-verbal communication. Non-verbal can be written, body language, approach i.e. showing confidence, Braille, sign language and many other ways that you will think of, or come across in your work.

You are also required to demonstrate that you have specific knowledge about the rights people have to communicate in their preferred method or language, and that you know your and your organisation's responsibilities regarding this. You can use 1 piece of evidence to cover more than 1 of the assessment criteria for each outcome. I have shown examples of this, although you will probably cover them differently i.e. I have covered assessment criteria 1-3 together but it may be easier for you to cover criteria 2- 4 together. Everybody's workplace activities are different and how you cover the outcomes and knowledge requirements will largely depend on you and the work activities you carry out.

Unit 051 Outcome one: - Understand why effective communication is important in the work setting

In this section you are asked to demonstrate understanding of why good communication is vital.

There are 2 assessment criteria which ask you to identify why people communicate and explain how the communication affects relationships.

The outcomes require you to produce evidence to show that you know how to speak, arrange environments and your own body language in order to make the individual feel secure, safe, and comfortable and un- intimidated when you or they are communicating information that is difficult, complicated or sensitive. You will also need to explain why this is important. Significant theories to be referred to may be around power dynamics and attachment as well as knowledge of the person and their relating patterns.

Environment will generally mean the room or area you are communicating in. It can mean even simple things like turning off a television to avoid distractions or making sure you have undisturbed privacy. It is always a good idea to read all the outcome requirements in a unit before you start to see where assessment criteria overlap. This way you can create evidence that entails the unit as a whole as well as the individual criteria.

You also need to show that you know where to access information regarding individuals communication preferences and needs, and that you are flexible to their changing needs.

Outcomes 2 wants you to **show** that you get information about individuals communication needs, that you use relevant methods of passing the information to others i.e. other staff, through handovers etc, that you can help the individual identify a variety of possible communication methods that would suit them and the people they are communicating with, and that you would provide any aids required in order for them to be able to communicate effectively.

You will also be able to show that you can consider and overcome barriers i.e do your team all need to be trained in sign language to meet a need? There is also a requirement that you can assess verbal and non-verbal communication and respond accordingly. As 3 of the 4 criteria ask you to demonstrate, this means much of the outcome will be covered through witness statements and direct observation.

You need to demonstrate here that you make sure the environment is suitable for communication (see above), that you make sure the individual has the support they need to be able to communicate (this could mean pen and paper, Braille or possibly another person to advocate for them.). You also need to show that you use appropriate ways of communicating to suit the individual

EXAMPLE – A new client arrives at the care home. The shift working has no real idea about the clients communication needs. You access their case history notes after asking for the required permission from your manager. In the clients notes it says that the client has difficulty speaking out about their needs, to staff she does not know and has been writing notes as a form of communication previously. You go to see the client to discuss their communication needs, and check they haven't changed. When you do this you take pen and paper in order to facilitate the communication using their preferred method. By talking to the client and reading what they write in response you help them identify that initially they will write notes but will try a new method of nodding and shaking their head to yes/no answers when the staff are in a hurry or are very busy. After the conversation you then go back to the staff room and pass on this information to staff through appropriate means i.e. handover book, communications book (say where you record the information, why, and who for).

N.B   Obviously when you write this you would right it in the first person i.e. I did this etc. If someone else was writing it they would say I witnessed * talking to a client and so on. You would also go into more specific detail than I have here. What I have written is just a general overview of what is being looked for.

Outcome 3 wants you to demonstrate other places that you can find out about communication and the different methods you communicate in. The criteria here suggest that you are communicating difficult messages or the communication will not be straight forward. (You are required to show evidence that you can communicate difficult and sensitive information in an appropriate and supportive way and that you can anticipate potential responses to information you communicate, and so prepare for them. Also, that you know when you need to seek help. This may be from other staff or the client's family or care team. Additionally you will need to be aware of barriers to communication and how to overcome them. The sign language example I gave earlier is applicable here but it could also be something as simple as your relationship with the client being a difficult one. Your Body language, tone of voice, the way you listen, talk, observe reactions to what you say and clear up any problems or misunderstandings. You will need to show that you know how to approach difficult communications and that you can support individuals who become distressed.
Knowledge of advocacy and how to access this for clients is vital also.

EXAMPLE- You have to tell a client that they can't go on the activity they had planned because of short staffing. In the past they have responded badly to changes in plans and so you talk to the clients case manager and key workers to decide the best approach to take when you tell them they won't be able to go out with staff.

N.B – You would go into more depth than I have written here.

Outcome 4- include information, to cover this outcome, about your responsibilities under the Anti Discrimination and Equal Opportunities Acts to help people communicate in their preferred method and language, as this will then be applicable to some of the knowledge specification requirements. Also make plenty of reference to confidentiality policies and procedures as you are required to demonstrate that you record details of sensitive and difficult communication in the right places and following confidentiality policies and legislation.

HSC51- UPDATE AND MAINTAIN RECORDS AND REPORTS

N.B- This is just a suggestion. Whenever you write about recording information and completing records about or for individuals find out about and try to mention the legislation and organisational policies that should be informing what you do. This will, on any unit, help with the knowledge requirements.

CONCLUSIONS- Unit 051 covers all the different ways you can communicate verbally and non-verbally and introduces you to Legislation and Organisational policies that should inform your practice. Although it is time consuming it is beneficial to read the legislation and policies. They contain important information that you will need to know for other units and that will improve your knowledge and practice in the workplace. By reading them you are ensuring that you get the most out of the Diploma qualification.

WHEN GATHERING EVIDENCE FOR UNITS BEAR IN MIND THE FOLLOWING. THAT WAY YOU WILL COVER KNOWLEDGE REQUIREMENTS WITHIN YOUR EVIDENCE.

VALUES- You need to demonstrate knowledge of individuals RIGHTS and legislation and organisational policies surrounding them. The Legislation and organisational policies will relate to things like: -

Equal opportunities
Human rights
Anti discrimination
Data protection
Disability
Confidentiality
Care Standards
Your organisations Statement of Purpose
Children's Act
Child protection
Mental Health Act
Deprivation of Liberties (DOLS)
Mental Capacity Act

Look at all the legislation and policies regarding the above areas and pick out the parts appropriate to each unit. Make sure you mention the laws and policies themselves as well though. I.e. The Anti Discrimination Act requires that I do not discriminate against people because of their language, creed, or communication preferences. Furthermore, it requires that I facilitate communication in via any method possible. You also need to show that you work within particular values which will be within your organisations policies and Statement of Purpose i.e 'to provide an integrated, ethical and inclusive service, which meets agreed needs and outcomes of people requiring health and/or social care.

LEGISLATION AND ORGANISATIONAL POLICY AND PROCEDURES

This section requires you to demonstrate that you know how the legislation and organisational policies relate to who is responsible and accountable for what in your workplace. For example, you are responsible for not behaving in a discriminating way but your manager would be accountable if there was found to be an ethos of discriminating behaviour in your workplace. They are also expected to supply all the tools/training etc required to promote anti discrimination and are accountable for this. You are responsible for using these tools and attending the required training.

THEORIES AND PRACTICE

This relates to your practice skills and specific models of working. Most of the information you require will be found in your organisations Statement of purpose. An example would be that your organisation favours an individualistic approach, (this is a model of working) therefore when you are working with those you care for you respect their different needs, preferences and wishes because you understand that everybody is different and has different needs.

UNIT 052: - ENGAGE IN PERSONAL DEVELOPMENT

UNIT 052 ENGAGE IN PERSONAL DEVELOPMENT

This unit is the one that most candidates struggle with. It requires you to reflect on your practice. This means that you need to show that you can look back on your practice and assess what was good about what you did or what you do, and what can be improved (develop your practice). Reflective practice is a highly regarded quality. It shows that you are willing to take account of your weaknesses as well as your strengths, and take action on them. You will get a lot of your evidence from this unit from your supervisions and various staff meetings, and also from your organisations appraisal system if you have one. Candidates often find this unit difficult because they are unaware that legislation even exists relating to their training and development.

This Unit has 5 outcomes.

Outcome 1 often confuses people straight away. Even when a candidate knows what they are being asked they often come to me baffled about how to cover it. A good example of how to cover Assessment Criteria 1 would be to use your job description to identify your role and responsibilities and to discuss this in supervision. You could ask your supervisor to write a witness statement detailing what you talked about, or ask your Assessor to observe the supervision. The criteria asks you to describe and explain which indicates a requirement for some written work. You will need to refer to standards of practice that influence your role and responsibilities i.e the Care standards Act outlines training requirements.

The second outcome is all about how you reflect on your practice. How you think about what you do and have done, in order to make changes, improve practice and for you to have an accurate assessment of what your strengths and weaknesses are. This is a useful tool to have, particularly when you are attending interviews. It shows you know yourself and are open to change, as well as being committed to your personal and professional development.

If you have an appraisal system then this can be used to help cover some of the criteria relating to it i.e. have your assessor sit in on your appraisal. If you can't use the appraisal system there is no reason why you can't set up a supervision with an informal appraisal as your agenda. Your assessor can then observe this. Within your appraisal/supervision you should discuss the criteria. An example can be as easy as you informing your supervisor that you have not had medicines training and that you feel it would boost your confidence and knowledge in this area. You have then identified your own need for improvement in an area, and how the need can be met. This will also be relevant to some criteria in outcome 3.

You will also need to think about how your own values and beliefs impact on your practice. How would you support a client to go to a Christian Fellowship if you are a Buddhist?

For Outcome 3 you will need to provide evidence about feedback you receive, the systems in place that support feedback and how you use this to develop. Again, the appraisal system would be useful evidence. Feedback may come from clients, staff, key workers, management, the client's family, and any other relevant people. Others with whom you work are usually therapists, social workers, teachers, consultants, managers etc. Constructive feedback can be as simple as explaining to a staff member how you approached a client about something difficult and the client responding badly. The staff member explains that the client does not respond to that way of working and makes suggestions for different approaches.

You will also need to demonstrate that you use the knowledge of standards discussed in Outcome 2 to inform your practice. i.e by attending training and using information learnt to enhance your practice.

Outcome 4
Candidates generally find it easiest to complete a work product for this describing the different support and supervision systems available within their organisation AND their function. These may include supervision, group supervision, mentors and other support that you may be able to identify. Each organisation offers different things. Support from outside organisations can include your union (all they require is for you to identify it as a possible form of support and how it can do so.). Some organisations have an outside facilitator who comes in and supervises the staff team as a whole on a regular basis for group supervision. Again this would be classed as an outside organisation being involved.

For other criteria in outcome 4 you are required to demonstrate (in other words provide evidence that you have used and do use) the identified systems to show you take responsibility for your own well-being, and to reflect on and identify ways to enhance your practice and meet set targets.

This could be something like discussing with your supervisor what you need to do to achieve promotion, or to improve your appraisal for the next yr. You will need to show how your supervisor or/and others support you to achieve your goal. This could be through passing on knowledge, setting tasks or you performing in an 'acting' role in a position senior to your own. It is expected that there would be regular reviews of how you are progressing towards your goals so you can identify what has helped and how, and discuss whether the tasks are appropriate for you to be able to reach your goal.

EXAMPLE: -

(WRITTEN AS A WITNESS STATEMENT BY THE CANDIDATES SUPERVISOR). * = Name

I witnessed * in supervision talking about her desire to develop within the organisation. As * supervisor I am aware that with some further development in her current role and some preparation * could apply for the Senior carer role coming up in 6 months. * is keen to work towards this opportunity. We identified a number of development opportunities that * could undertake in order for her to reach this goal. These are: -

- For * to regularly run shifts. I as * supervisor will put this in place for her.
- For * to begin her Diploma 4. Through this she will begin to build up the knowledge and skills appropriate for a senior member of staff.
- * to be mentored by one of the current seniors who has vast enough experience to impart knowledge and practice

* and I have been reviewing her progress on a regular basis (monthly). * identified in 1 of the reviews that running shifts was useful, but she felt there was more to the role than she was learning, and she was unsure of how to deal with and follow correct procedures in certain situations. As * said that the mentoring was going well and felt she was learning a lot we identified shift leading skills that * mentor could take her through….. and so on.

In this example mentoring, shift leading and Diploma have been development opportunities that will enhance knowledge and practice. The Senior position is also a development opportunity. Because you are discussing working towards a

Senior post this is seen as focusing on your continual development. The supervisor should refer to records and reviews of your progress and explains briefly the confidentiality and data protection procedures around this. A review of the targets and goals would fulfil requirements for Outcome 5.

The knowledge requirement for this unit is short, but people often get stuck. Find your workplaces copy of the Care standards 2000 and refer to it for guidance.

VALUES- the rights of yourself and others relating to improving your knowledge and practice. The idea of other people's rights regarding your development confuses lots of candidates and also the idea of this creating dilemmas and conflicts in your practice. Think about the following: -

THOSE THAT YOU CARE FOR HAVE THE RIGHT TO HAVE FULLY TRAINED AND QUALIFIED STAFF, AND TO HAVE A CERTAIN STANDARD OF CARE. THIS IS COVERED BY CHILD PROTECTION/POVA, HUMAN RIGHTS ACT, CHILDRENS ACT, CARE STANDARDS 2000.

YOU HAVE THE RIGHT TO RECEIVE SPECIFIC JOB RELATED TRAINING INCLUDING MANDATORY TRAINING I.E. MEDICINES, HEALTH AND SAFETY, CHILD PROTECTION/POVA, IN ORDER FOR YOU TO CARE APPROPRIATELY, EFFECTIVELY AND SAFELY SEE CARE STANDARDS ACT 2000, EQUAL OPPURTUNITIES ACT, ANTI DISCRIMINATION ACT. REMEMBER THERE IS ALSO NOW LEGISLATION IN PLACE RELATING TO DIPLOMA. DIPLOMA 2/3 IS NOW A MANDATORY GOVERNMENT REQUIREMENT.

LEGISLATION AND ORGANISATIONAL POLICY AND PROCEDURES – The legislation listed under values and the related organisational policies (your workplace should have a policy relating to staff development.) should give you the information you require for this knowledge specification. You should show that you know who is responsible and accountable for what, relating to your personal and professional development. I.e. your supervisor may be responsible for your appraisal, you are responsible for turning up to and completing training, your manager is accountable and responsible for making sure that all staff have completed mandatory training. Demonstrate that you are aware of the legislation and organisational policies relating to you being able to access training and meet your personal and professional development needs. You will find the legislation requirement information in the list that I gave earlier under values i.e. the equal opportunities act states that you should be given equal access to training and development opportunities as anyone else.

Demonstrate knowledge of the arrangements for your supervision and appraisal. When, where and the purpose.

THEORY AND PRACTICE – Where do you access information and knowledge about best practice and relevant skills for your workplace and the people you work with or care for.

What does the legislation and the organisational policies say is the reason for focusing on staff development? Why do they say you must undertake mandatory training? Think again about the information I wrote about yours and others rights regarding your training that I wrote about in the values section.

You should show you have accessed **a number of different sources** for help, advice and support in order to enable your development. Individuals and key people can be supervisors, mentors, therapists, social workers, consultants, other experts and outside training organisations.

Identify how you can take your knowledge and skills to different places. This can include your mandatory training which would be valid in any caring workplace. Think about the way you work with clients, i.e. treating them in a non-discriminating way, and explain how you would continue to work that way in another work environment.

CONCLUSIONS- Candidates do often struggle with this unit. We think a lot about the work we do but our own personal and professional development rights and requirements is not something we generally think about in any depth. Or we may think about where we are going, but not about how we get there. This unit should make us think, however, about our rights to training and the rights that those we care for have to receive quality staff that are fully trained.

Unit 053- Promote Equality and Inclusion

INTRODUCTION

Unit 053 (SHC 33) is all focused on your awareness of legislation and policies in regards to Equality, Diversity and Inclusion. Additionally, you must DEMONSTRATE how you implement the legislation and policies into your practice.
There are 3 learning outcomes for the unit.

OUTCOME 1

Outcome 1 checks your understanding of the terms Diversity, Equality and Inclusion and asks you to describe and explain how the terms can impact on practice. There are 3 assessment criteria for you to complete for this outcome.

Evidence for this unit could be a work product such as an essay. Alternatively you could complete an answer and question session with your assessor and/or gather some witness testimonies.

You will need to look up the Equality, Diversity and Inclusion policies in your workplace and check your understanding of the key terms.

You will need to be able to describe a lack of awareness of or adherence to policies and legislation for Equality, Diversity and Inclusion can lead to discrimination. Then in Outcome 3 how awareness can promote Equality and Diversity.

*EXAMPLE**

Equality- Recognising that we are all equal, but that some individuals (i.e your service users) may require assistance to be treated equally, and are vulnerable to discrimination because they are service users. This may be because they are disabled, care leavers etc.

Diversity- Recognising difference rather than ignoring it. Respecting difference in culture, religion or maybe just different methods of practicing.

Awareness and understanding of the above leads to inclusion.

Ignorance of the above can lead to vulnerable service users being marginalised, ignored or treated differently. This is Discrimination.

Many work places insist workers now have Equality and Diversity training. If you have a certificate for this then include it in your portfolio.

OUTCOME 2

For this outcome you will be expected to go into further and more explicit detail about how the legislation applies to your practice. If you have written something quite detailed for Outcome 1 then you may have enough evidence already for Assessment criteria 1.
For Assessment criteria 2 you will need to provide specific examples and produce witness testimonies and/or Direct observations to back up what you can say.
Examples of these might be ensuring a service user can attend their chosen place of worship although you practice a different religion. Or maybe you help a service user access school or training.

OUTCOME 3

There are 3 assessment criteria for outcome 3 which ask you to demonstrate how you are a role model for others, how you support others and how you would challenge others.
The first 2 assessment criteria ask you to demonstrate and so you will require observed evidence through Witness testimony or direct observation.
The 3rd criteria allows for the possibility that you may not have had need to challenge discrimination, by asking you to explain how you would. This can be achieved via a work product or question and answering session with your assessor.
Role modelling for others can be covered by providing examples of when you have explicitly carried out tasks to ensure service users are treated in an inclusive way. Maybe you supported a service user by attending their statutory review to ensure they were heard or to advocate for them.
Supporting others to do this may be as simple as inducting a new team member and showing them the related policies, emphasising their importance and letting them know they are an important part of how you practice.

You might. For example, have said to them that client x attends a Mosque at the weekend and some staff struggle with this as they have different religious beliefs. You might have explained to the new team member why it is important to facilitate the client's wishes but how to do this in a way that acknowledges others religious beliefs are different. You may have talked to them about how personal values sometimes impact on our working practice and so why it is important to be aware of them.

Challenging discrimination can be difficult, especially if it is an organisational problem. You should be able to explain the process you would go down and how it links to legislation and policies. There are, however, smaller but just as significant ways, in which we might challenge discrimination.

Example*

Client x is 18 and wants a staff member to go to the pub with her. Staff member y approaches you and says she would not take her own 18yr old to the pub so why client x. Conversation should take place about our own personal values and the difference between our own children and those who are vulnerable and who may need support to try out activities that our own children could manage safely alone.
i.e I wouldn't take my own 18yr old to the pub. This is because they have friends they can go with. I know they will be safe. I know they will get a lift home. I know they won't go off with strangers. I have taught them how to be safe. Client x is vulnerable to approaches from strangers, to binge drinking. They need to be helped to learn the skills of an 18 yr old in a supported way.

VALUES

Having an awareness of others differences and their rights to certain things. Practicing reflectively. Being aware of your own personal values and how these can impact on your practice.
Supporting those who could be subject to discrimination to access their rights.

LEGISLATION AND ORGANISATIONAL POLICIES AND PROCEDURES

UN Convention on Children's Rights 1989

Children Act 1989 Children Act 2004 (Children's Services) Regulations 2005

Protection of Children Act 1999/ Leaving Care Act 2000/ Adoption and Children Act 2002

Education Acts 1921, 1944, 1970, 1981, 1988, 2002

Special Educational Needs and Disability Act 2001

Carers (Equal Opportunities) Act 2004/ Carers (Recognition and Services) Act 1995

Human Rights Act 1998

Race Relations Act 1976 and Race Relations (Amendments) Act 2000 and 2003

Sex Discrimination Act 1975 and 1986

Disability Discrimination Act 1995

Disabled Persons Act 1944-1986/ Chronically Sick and Disabled Act 1970. Carers and Disabled Children Act 2000

Access to Health Care Records Act 2000/ Access to Personal Files Act 1987

Data Protection Act 1984 and 1998/ Freedom of Information Act 2000

THEORIES AND PRACTICE

Examples of the impact of Discrimination. Examples of difference made to people's lives through inclusivity.
Does your organisation have a mandatory training requirement for Equality and Diversity?
How much emphasis is placed on Equality and Diversity in staff inductions?
Reflective practice and challenging personal values.
Knowledge of and awareness of the potential for Institutional discrimination.

Unit 054- PRINCIPLES FOR IMPLEMENTING DUTY OF CARE

Unit 054 requires you to have an understanding of what safe practice is and to be able to demonstrate that you know when you have a duty to take actions to protect the clients you work with (Duty of care).
This may mean protecting your clients from themselves or from others.
There are 3 learning outcomes for this unit.

OUTCOME 1- Understand how Duty of Care contributes to safe practice

This outcome asks you to explain your understanding for both assessment criteria. Therefore questioning and answering with your assessor or a work product should suffice.
Tip- the Questioning and answering method will reduce your workload.

Assessment criteria 1 asks you to explain what duty of care means for you in your practice.
In short it is about identifying problems and knowing whether you or someone else needs to act on them.

Example: You see a member of staff hit a client.

Q. What do you need to do and when?
A. Report it to a Senior member of staff straight away.

Q. Why?
A. Because the action is classed as abuse?

Q. How do you know this?
A. Child protection and POVA training, policies and legislation tell me it is abuse.

When the event happened you knew you had to do something and used the policies, training and legislation resources you had to take correct action. This is understanding and fulfilling your Duty of Care.

Assessment criteria 2 asks you to explain how duty of care contributes to safe practice.
The example in criteria 1 highlights how knowing and fulfilling your duty of care can help prevent abuse. If you had ignored the incident it may have happened

again and you would possibly have been contributing to a growing culture of abuse within your organisation.

Use your own example and ask yourself the questions in the example given. Then ask yourself what might happen if you did not follow procedure, policy and legislation guidelines.
If you can come up with the answers you have sufficient understanding and knowledge to meet this outcome.

OUTCOME 2- addressing conflicts between individuals rights and your duty of care.

There are 3 assessment criteria which all ask you to describe or explain. Again, Question and answering would be a good choice to save you from completing lots of written work for a work product.
The legislation in this area is becoming more and more prominent but this is necessary as it is not alright to control what clients can and can't do because we don't agree (own personal values).
We must respect their choices while protecting them from harm. Protecting them from harm ALWAYS comes first but you may need to assess a clients capacity to make their own decisions Below is an example:

Q. A 16yr old wants to smoke.

A. I know that smoking will do them harm and I don't agree with it.

But they have the right to make their own choices?

   A. Yes they do so…

Do they understand the harm smoking does? If not then your Duty of care means you should explain it to them.

   A. Yes they do. Then they can make their own decision.

However….

Your Duty of care would mean you should not purchase them cigarettes. You cannot stop the client from accessing them themselves though.

But additionally:

What if smoking cigarettes puts them at risk in other ways? For example, they tell you that when they next have a cigarette they are going to abscond and you are aware they have been feeling suicidal.

You have a duty of care to protect!! This might mean stopping them from having the cigarette or heavily supervising them while they are outside smoking.

In addition to this there can be added complications. If the person was 15yrs, for example, parental responsibility would mean having to ask a parent or the responsible person their views.

Not allowing a client may increase their risk to self and/or others? Will they become violent?

Complicated!!!! Yes!!!!

Asking yourself the following questions may help:

1. What is the risk if I allow the activity?
2. What is the risk if I don't allow the activity?
3. What rights does the young person have?
4. What legislation and policies support this?
5. Who else has a say? What rights do they have?
6. What legislation and policies support this?
7. Is Mental capacity an issue at present?
8. What if it was at some point? How would it change things?

Asking yourself these questions would be called doing a risk assessment.

Written risk assessments are useful means of measuring risk and rights in order to come to satisfactory outcomes. They must be updated regularly and take into account known potential changes based on the clients history. Otherwise they will not be effective.

The last assessment criteria asks you to explain where you would get help and advice. Below is a list of just some of the places. You may not have all of these in your workplace:

Supervision
Shift leader
Manager
Risk assessment
Legislation
Policies
Careplans
Social Worker
Nurse
Psychiatrist
Psychologist
Psychotherapist
Occupational therapist.

OUTCOME 3- Responding to complaints

Sometimes complaints and allegations get mixed up. Knowing the difference is vital.

There are:

Complaints. All complaints should be investigated and responded to. Your organisation should have a policy specifying guidelines.

Complaints that are investigated and become allegations.

Allegations

Examples- A complaint

Client X wanted to go to the cinema.

Q. Does this mean she missed out on a right?

A. Could be argued the client has a right to socialise with others so yes?

An investigation should take place.

Note- An investigation is not necessarily a big thing. It may be as simple as asking the shift leader what happened.

The shift leader is asked what happened. The trip could not be facilitated as there was an incident with another client and this meant a staff member was not available to take Client X to the cinema. Client X's risk assessment states she cannot go alone due to risk factors.
Duty of care to other clients and Client X override right to socialise.

Complaints that lead to allegation-

Client X complains that she was hurt during a restraint.

On investigation one of the staff involved says the other staff member involved seemed angry during the restraint and that they used a unauthorised technique. This led to Client x being injured.

This is now an allegation of abuse.

Allegations-

Client X says the staff have not fed her all week.

This is an allegation as it is denial of a basic need to live, which is classed as abuse.

It is important that you are clear about the difference between the 3. If you are ever unsure speak to your manager. It is better to be safe than sorry. If the complaint is about your manager seek advice from their line manager.

Make sure you understand the complaints policy. Is there specific paperwork that should be used by someone making a complaint?

What are your responsibilities and time frames? What are the responsibilities and time frames for others to respond to the complaint?

Knowing the above information, who should be involved and the time frames for response will cover assessment criteria 2.

VALUES

Rights of others to be protected

Rights to be protected versus right to make own choices

Awareness of personal values and how these can impact on decision making
Legislation

SEE LIST AT END OF THE BOOK. ALL APPLY ALONGSIDE THE RELEVENT POLICIES IN THE WORKPLACE.

Theories and practice

Risk assessment
Reflective practice
Problem solving techniques
Rights and responsibilities

SECTION 7- LEGISLATION

CURRENT LEGISLATION

Fire Precautions Act 1971

Reporting of Injuries, Diseases and Dangerous Occurrences Regulations 1995 (RIDDOR)

Health And Safety of Work Act 1974

Manual Handling Operations Regulation 1992

Control Of Substances Hazardous to Health regulation 2002 (COSHH)

UN Convention on Children's Rights 1989

Children Act 1989 Children Act 2004 (Children's Services) Regulations 2005

Protection of Children Act 1999/ Leaving Care Act 2000/ Adoption and Children Act 2002

Education Acts 1921, 1944, 1970, 1981, 1988, 2002

Special Educational Needs and Disability Act 2001

Mental Health Act 1983 and 2007 amended Act

NHS and Community Care Act 1990

.Carers (Equal Opportunities) Act 2004/ Carers (Recognition and Services) Act 1995

Care Standards Act 2000

Health and Safety at Work Act 1974

Family Allowance Act 1945/ National Insurance Act 1946/ National Health Service Act 1948/ National Assistance Act 1948

Human Rights Act 1998

Race Relations Act 1976 and Race Relations (Amendments) Act 2000 and 2003

Sex Discrimination Act 1975 and 1986

Disability Discrimination Act 1995

Disabled Persons Act 1944-1986/ Chronically Sick and Disabled Act 1970. Carers and Disabled Children Act 2000

Access to Health Care Records Act 2000/ Access to Personal Files Act 1987

Data Protection Act 1984 and 1998/ Freedom of Information Act 2000

Crime and Disorder Act 1998

FINAL CONCLUSIONS- The Diploma is hard work. Not because it is necessarily difficult (especially now that you have read this) but because it is time consuming, mandatory and lets face it slightly tedious at times. I have had candidates who have dragged out their Diploma over months because they hate doing it so much. My advice would be to just do it. Get it over with. The candidates that approach it this way are the ones who produce the best quality work and who finish quicker. By getting on with it you are also showing your employers that you are committed to your personal and professional development and are prepared to take on tasks that you don't enjoy because you understand their importance and relevance. **GOOD LUCK !!!!!!!!!!!!!!!**

3553074R00031

Printed in Great Britain
by Amazon.co.uk, Ltd.,
Marston Gate.